The crocodile is like a giant lizard. It is a member of the animal family called reptiles. There were even larger reptiles thousands of years ago.

TO OUR ANCESTORS

A crocodile can grow to 20 feet long!

A crocodile's huge mouth has more than 65 teeth, which are large, hard and very sharp.

OCO

he toothpaste for everyone.

During most of the day, the crocodile floats with only its nose and eyes above the water. It looks like it's asleep.

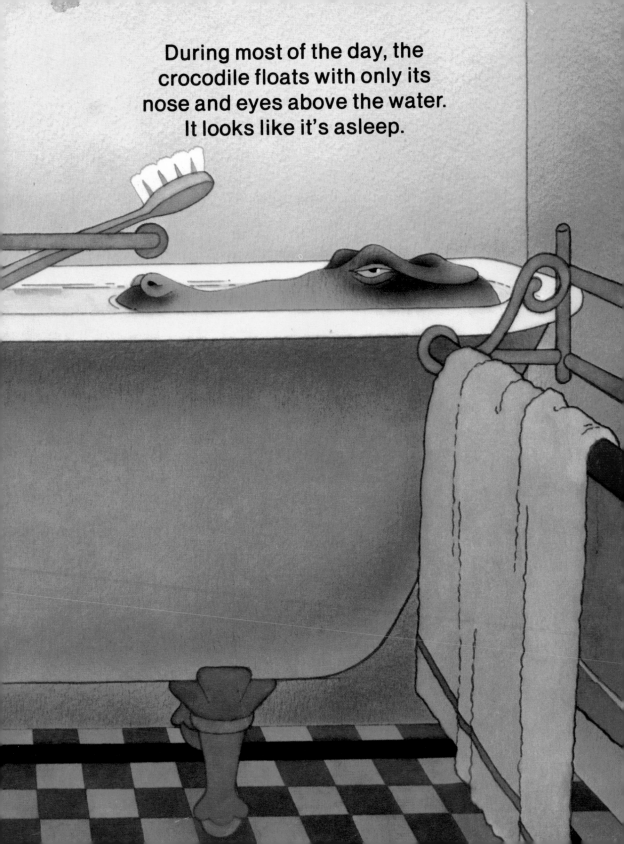

Usually, the crocodile looks for
food only after dark.

The crocodile moves slowly on land,
but it can swim fast in the water.

PIRANHAS & CARP

Baby crocodiles usually eat bugs.
Adult crocodiles like fish, but they
also eat birds and other animals.

TSE TSE FLIES

MOSQUITOS

GRASSHOPPERS

WORMS

ANTS

SODA WATER

TROPICAL WATER

Skin from the crocodile's stomach is used to make shoes and purses.

A crocodile's back and tail are protected by hard scales.

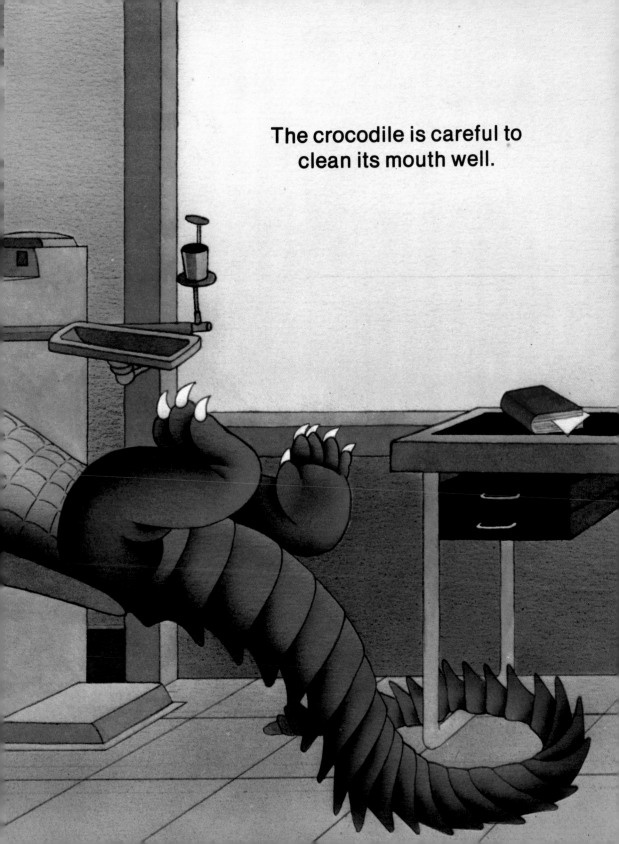

The crocodile is careful to clean its mouth well.

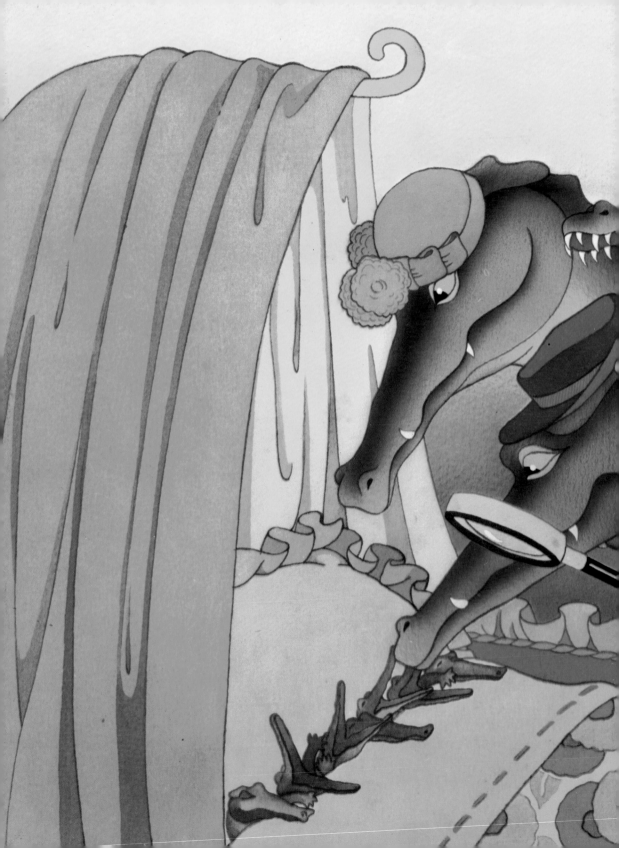